Contents

The first part of this book tells you the story of
Mohandas Gandhi.
The second part tells you how we can find out
about his life.

Childhood

Mohandas Gandhi was born in India in 1869, about 130 years ago. When he was a little boy, he was afraid of the dark. He always slept with a night-light.

Gandhi's family were **Hindus**. When he was thirteen he had an **arranged marriage**. He did not choose his wife. He and his wife **Kasturbai** did not live together until they were adults.

Work

In 1888, when he was nineteen, Gandhi went to London to learn how to be a **lawyer**. He was often lonely and homesick for India. He missed his wife **Kasturbai**.

In 1893 Gandhi went to work in
South Africa. One day, he was thrown
off a train because another passenger
hated Indians.

Fighting racism

This **racism** made Gandhi angry.
He began to fight racism, but peacefully.
One day, he stopped police horses
charging at a crowd by making everyone
lie on the ground. He knew that the horses
would not want to step on people.

In 1915 Gandhi went home to India. Many people had heard of his good work. When his boat landed at Bombay he was treated like a hero. He was nicknamed '**Mahatma**' meaning 'Great Soul'.

Britain ruled India

Britain **ruled** over India at the time. Many Indians did not like this. In 1919 British soldiers shot a crowd of 400 peaceful **protestors.** Gandhi believed that British rule had to end.

Gandhi became a great leader for the
Indian people. He ran many peaceful
meetings to show the British that they
should leave India and stop ruling there.

Trying to change things

In 1931 Gandhi went to Britain to talk to the Prime Minister. He agreed with many of Gandhi's ideas, but still said that the British would not leave India.

When he got home to India, Gandhi was arrested for trying to change things. During his life he spent a total of seven years in prison. He passed the time thinking and spinning cotton.

Independence

On 15 August 1947, the British left India. India became **independent**. The Indian flag could at last be raised. This huge country was then split into two countries, India and Pakistan.

Many people all over the world loved
Gandhi and had agreed with his ideas
to make India independent. Yet on
January 30, 1948, a gunman killed him
as he went to pray.

Funeral

Gandhi's last words were 'Hay Rama'. This means 'Oh God'. The Indian prime minister said, 'The light has gone out of our lives.'

One million people went to Gandhi's funeral. He was India's greatest leader. His ideas are still admired and needed today.

Photographs

This photograph shows Gandhi when he was seven. He was a shy boy. His mother was very religious and taught him to always be truthful and think of others.

Gandhi was **vegetarian**. This photograph shows him in London in 1890 with members of a vegetarian club where he made friends. He is in the bottom row, on the right.

In London and South Africa, Gandhi wore a smart suit. When he was 44 he decided to dress simply, like most Indians at the time.

Gandhi was very popular with ordinary
people. This photo shows him laughing
and joking with factory workers in Britain
in 1931.

Reports and artefacts

This news report from an American newspaper is about Gandhi's **fasting**. It shows that he was ready to starve himself to death to get laws changed.

The New York Times.

Copyright, 1932, by The New York Times Company.

NEW YORK, WEDNESDAY, SEPTEMBER 21, 1932   **** +   TW

d as Second-Class Matter,
ffice, New York, N. Y.

M'KEE SAYS BANKERS FORCE BUDGET CUTS; DR. NORRIS RESIGNS

Loans to Stop if $80,000,000 Is Not Slashed, Aid Pledged for Public Works if It Is.

MAYOR ACCEPTS ULTIMATUM

"Determined to Get Economy, He Repeats—Office Working Nights to Rush Schedules.

NORRIS QUITS IN PROTEST

Medical Examiner Resents 20% Cut for Bureau—City Gets Offer for Model Housing Development.

Forging ahead yesterday toward budget economy as a means of obtaining further loans from the bank-

CURRY AND M'COOEY

Gandhi, Tired and Ill, Begins His Death Fast After Hearty Meal and Prayer for Strength

Wireless to The New York Times.

BOMBAY, Sept. 20. — Mahatma Gandhi solemnly began his "fast unto death" today behind the walls of Yerovda jail at Poona.

Exhausted by the strain of the past few days, the 63-year-old Mahatma was ill and under a doctor's care as he started his fateful hunger strike. He has had heavy correspondence and a colossal number of telegrams to deal with ever since he announced he would starve to death as a protest against the government's communal settlement. In view of his condition, the prison physician decided not to allow visitors to see him this morning.

All over India Hindus ceased work. Thousands went to the temples to pray for the Mahatma. Other thousands shuttered their shops or stayed away from their work at the factories as a gesture of sorrow.

Mr. Gandhi had a substantial meal before beginning his long, slow ordeal. He had his usual dates, soaked in water, and with them he ate whole-meal bread, tomatoes, oranges and curd. Then, visibly agitated, his secretary, Mahadev Desai, handed him a glass of lemon juice and soda.

This was the last sustenance he will touch, except for water.

When his last meal was finished, the Mahatma quietly announced his fast had started, and knelt to pray, with Vallabhai Patel, the All-India Nationalist Congress leader, and Mr. Desai kneeling alongside him.

A strangely subdued tension gripped the big Hindu centres of India as his fast began. Bombay's Hindu business quarters were deserted. The cotton and bullion markets and the Stock Exchange were closed. Nineteen cotton mills had to suspend because their workers failed to appear. Many schools and colleges were forced to shut their doors because so few students reported for classes. In the European and Moslem quarters, however, business went on as usual without interference.

The most significant event of the day was the admission of the "untouchables" for the first time to certain Hindu temples in Bombay, Nasik and Ahmedabad.

Despite the opposition of the ortho-

Continued on Page Eight.

FINDS RACKETS COST

LA FOLLETTE BEATEN IN WISCONSIN FIGHT; DR. LOVE LOSES HERE

Kohler, Conservative, Named for Governor—Youngman Leads in Bay State.

MRS. PRATT WINS IN CITY

McCooey Man Defeats Dr. Love in State Senate Race—Hastings Renominated.

MIX-UP OVER BALLOTS HERE

Patrolman and Boy Are Shot in Dispute at Polls—Roosevelt Scores Victory Up-State.

Voters in New York, Massachusetts and Wisconsin went to the polls yesterday for the last of the State

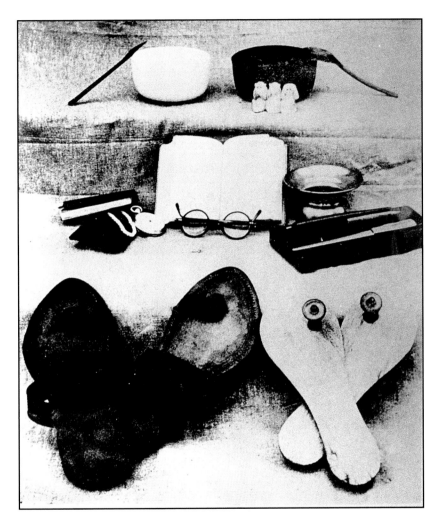

Gandhi believed in living simply. This picture shows the few things he owned when he died. They were only worth about £2.50.

Glossary

This glossary explains difficult words, and helps you to say words which may be hard to say.

arranged marriage many **Hindus** marry someone who is chosen by their parents. This is called an arranged marriage

artefacts things which people make and use, like tools, clothes and cooking pots. We can learn about the past by looking at old artefacts. You say *arty-facts*

fasting not eating anything

Hindu many Indians follow the Hindu religion, which is one of the main world religions. Hindus believe that if you lead a good life, you will be re-born as a better person. You say *hin-doo*

independent free

Kasturbai you say *kast-ur-by*

lawyer person who has studied law, which is all the rules that people should follow in a country

protester someone who shows publicly that they disagree with something, usually a rule

Mahatma you say *ma-hat-ma*

Mohandas you say *mo-han-das*

racism hating somebody just because they are from a different country or have a different colour of skin

rule be in control

vegetarian someone who doesn't eat meat or fish

Index